Broccoli Hair

Kristen Scott

13TH & JOAN

13th & Joan books may be purchased for educational, business or sales promotional use. For information, please email the Sales Department at sales@13thandjoan.com.

Printed in the U.S. A.

First Printing

10   9   8   7   6   5   4   3   2   1

Library of Congress Cataloging-in-Publication Data has been applied for.
ISBN 978-1-953156-35-8

Broccoli
Hair

A book written from personal inspiration. *Broccoli Hair* was brought to life to encourage self-love. We are all born different and that is what makes each of us unique. Loving yourself from the inside out promotes power and confidence no one should touch. I hope you love this book and yourself as much as I do.

Love Always,
Kristen

Awake again a new day.

Time to do my hair so I can slay.

Mommy gets the spray, the brush, the comb.

She's going to do my hair so I can leave home.

A pony, some braids, maybe even a *twist*. I ask,

"Can it be free? Just add some mist!"

I love, *I love* my broccoli hair.
Curls, natural, *this beauty I wear.*

Mommy looks at me with joy and *delight!*
"I love your broccoli hair, too.

Let's do it just right."

We condition, untangle, and moisturize.
My broccoli hair is perfect...*just the right size.*

I look in the mirror. So *proud* of it all.
Each coil and curl, *the big and the small.*

My broccoli hair, it is a part of me
I'm fierce and I'm powerful.
Love yourself...that's the key!

My Broccoli Hair Affirmation

I am beautiful inside and out.
I am enough.
I love all of me!

Kristen Scott is an Entrepreneur and Philanthropist born and raised in New Orleans, Louisiana. Graduating with honors from Louisiana State University, she excelled in her career as a Pharmaceutical Representative before becoming an author. After marrying her husband, the couple had a beautiful daughter, *Kenzi,* who became *Broccoli Hair's* inspiration.

Dear Reader,

It is important that we learn to express the ways that we are proud to be who we are. Practice answering the questions below to remind you of your inner beauty.

Love,
Kristen

Are you *proud* of yourself?

What do you *like* most about yourself?

Do you like *helping* others? Why?

What makes you *different*?

How would you describe *yourself*?

What is something *you* can teach others?

What is your *superpower*?

Connect with the Author

Instagram: @mrskristenscott
Twitter: @MrsKristenScott
Facebook: Kristen Scott

CPSIA information can be obtained
at www.ICGtesting.com
Printed in the USA
LVHW071435050422
715391LV00007B/57